A Child's Treasury of Best-Loved
PRAYERS

This book is a gift for

_____

from

_____

A Child's Treasury of Best-Loved PRAYERS

Illustrated by Teddy Edinjiklian

This book is dedicated to my late parents, Agavni and Abraham Edinjiklian. I will cherish their memories as long as I live. – T.E.

ISBN 978-1-60261-221-1

Book design by Miles Parsons

Printed in China

Table of Contents

Each Morning When I Wake

Each morning when I wake I say
Take care of me, dear Lord, today.
In work and play, please let me be
Always, Jesus, just for thee.
In all I think, do, and say
Take care of me, dear God, I pray.

Amen

5

Good Morning, Dear God

Good morning, dear God, I offer you
My thoughts, words, and actions
And all that I do.

Amen

Love of Jesus

Love of Jesus fill us.
Holy Spirit guide us.
Will of the Father be done.

Amen

Oh, Jesus, I Give You Today

Oh, Jesus, I give you today all that I think and do and say.
Oh, Jesus, I love you and pray more love today than yesterday.
Oh, God, be with me, I pray, be by my side forever to stay.

Amen

Angel of God

Angel of God, my guardian dear,
To whom His love commits me here,
Ever this day, be at my side,
To light and guard
To rule and guide.

Amen

Heart of Jesus

Heart of Jesus, I adore.
Heart of Mary, I implore.
Heart of Joseph, meek and just.
In these three hearts I place my trust.

Amen

The Gift

What can I give him,
Poor as I am;
If I were a shepherd,
I'd give him a lamb,
If I were a wise man,
I would do my part.
But what can I give him?
I will give him my heart.

—Christina Rossetti

Song of Thanks

Oh, the Lord is good to me,
And so I thank the Lord,
For giving me the things I need,
The sun, and the rain, and the apple seed,
Oh, the Lord is good to me.

Amen

14

All Blessings

Praise God from whom all blessings flow;
Praise him all Creatures here below;
Praise him above, ye heavenly host;
Praise Father, Son, and Holy Ghost.

Amen

All Things Bright and Beautiful

All things bright and beautiful,
All creatures great and small,
All things wise and wonderful,
The Lord God made them all.

Amen

Thank You for Everything

Thank you for the world so sweet;
Thank you for the food we eat;
Thank you for the birds that sing;
Thank you, God, for everything.

Amen

Father We Thank You

Father, we thank You for the night,
And for the pleasant morning light,
For rest and food and loving care,
And all that makes the day so fair.
Help us to do the things we should,
To be to others kind and good;
In all we do and all we say,
To grow more loving every day.

Amen

18

My Prayer

Dear Lord, for these three things I pray:
To know you more clearly,
To love you more dearly,
To follow you more nearly,
Every day.

Amen

Bless Us, O Lord

Bless us, O Lord, and these Your gifts,
Which we are about to receive from Your bounty
Through Christ our Lord.

Amen

A Prayer of Thanksgiving

We thank thee, Lord,
For Happy Hearts,
For rain and sunny weather;
We thank thee, Lord
For this our food
And that we are together.

Amen

Our Daily Bread

God is great,
God is good,
And we thank Him
For our food.
By His hands
We are fed,
Thank you, Lord,
For our daily bread.

Amen

Invitation to Jesus

Lord Jesus, be our holy Guest,
Our morning joy, our evening rest;
And with our daily bread impart
Thy love and peace in every heart.

Amen

Thank You, Father

Heavenly Father, thanks we say
For the food we have today,
May there be enough to share,
With other people everywhere.

Amen

Praise and Blessings

For food and all Thy gifts of love
We give Thee thanks and praise,
Look down, O Father, from above,
And bless us all our days.

Amen

Protect Us, Lord

Lord, keep us safe this night,
Secure from all our fears.
May angels guard us while we sleep,
Till morning light appears.

Amen

Now I Lay Me Down to Sleep

Now I lay me down to sleep;
I pray the Lord my soul to keep.
Watch over me through the night,
And wake me with the morning light.

Amen

God Bless

I see the moon,
And the moon sees me.
God bless the moon,
And God bless me.

Amen

32